Patterns

The Scribbles Institute™ *Young Artist Basics*

Published by The Child's World®
PO Box 326
Chanhassen, MN 55317-0326
800-599-READ
www.childsworld.com

Design and Production: The Creative Spark, San Juan Capistrano, CA
Series Editor: Elizabeth Sirimarco Budd

Photos:
© David M. Budd Photography: Cover, 14, 19
© Brandon D. Cole/CORBIS: 22
© 2002 Cordon Art B.V. - Baarn - Holland. All rights reserved.: 17
© Corel Corporation: 12-13, 21
© D. Robert Franz/CORBIS: 23
© National Portrait Gallery, Smithsonian Institution/Art Resource, NY: 30
© The Newark Museum/Art Resource, NY: 25, 28
© 2002 Estate of Pablo Picasso/Artists Rights Society (ARS), New York/David
    Heald©The Soloman R. Guggenheim Foundation, New York: 21
© Scala/Art Resource, NY: 8
© Michel Zabe/Art Resource, NY: 11

Library of Congress Cataloging-in-Publication Data
Court, Robert, 1956–
  Patterns / by Rob Court.
      p. cm. — (Young artists basics series)
Includes index.
Summary: Simple text and "Loopi the Fantastic Line" describe the concept
of patterns, how they differ, and their role in art and architecture.
  ISBN 1-56766-079-7 (alk. paper)
  1. Line (Art)—Juvenile literature. 2. Drawing—Technique—Juvenile literature.
3. Decoration and ornament—Juvenile literature. 4. Art appreciation—Juvenile
appreciation. [1. Line (Art) 2. Pattern perception. 3. Drawing—Technique. 4.
Decoration and ornament, Architectural.] I. Title. II. Series.
  NC754 .C68 2002
  701'.8—dc21
                                              2002005555

Patterns

Rob Court

The
Child's
World

Loopi is a line,
a fantastic line.

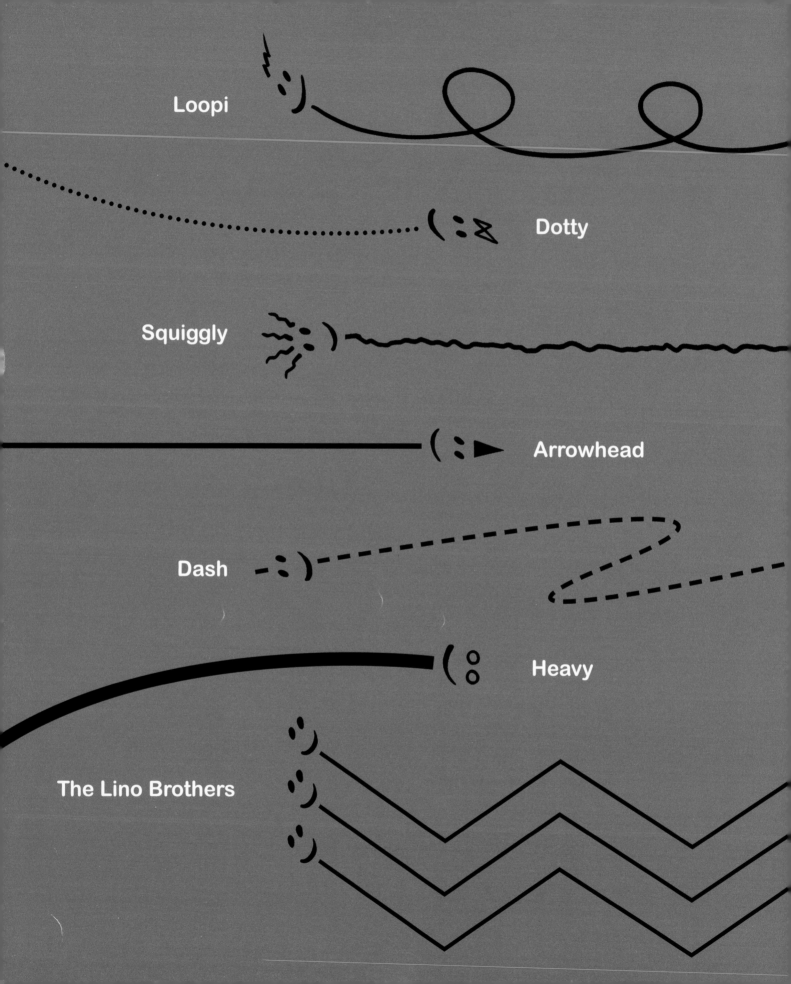

There are many kinds of lines.

Some are dotted lines.

Some are squiggly lines.

Some lines point in a direction.

Some lines are drawn with dashes.

Other lines are very, very thick.

Sometimes lines work together
to make patterns.

Patterns are repeated shapes and colors that make a **design.** People have used lines to make patterns since ancient times. Egyptians repeated blue and gold lines to make a beautiful **sculpture** for a king.

The sculpture in this picture was made more than 2,300 years ago. Artists created it in honor of an Egyptian king named Tutankhamen. Can you see where the artists repeated lines to make patterns?

Can you find Heavy in the picture? Is he showing you a pattern made with straight lines or curved lines?

Hundreds of years ago, Native Americans known as the Maya lived in Mexico. Mayan artists made the mask shown here. Can you see the patterns they made with colored stones?

Many of the stones are square. Can you see which stones are large and which are small? If you could touch the mask, how do you think it would feel?

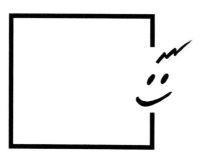

11

You can see a pattern when windows are repeated on the wall of a building. Ancient Romans used **arches** to make windows.

A curved line can make an arch.

The Colosseum in Rome, Italy, was built nearly 2,000 years ago. Can you see the patterns made with curved lines? Can you see the patterns made with straight lines?

13

You can see patterns on buildings. Sometimes walls are made with bricks that are shaped like rectangles. Together, many bricks can make a pattern.

The Lino Brothers help you to see patterns in the wall. A rectangle is a shape with two short sides and two long sides. Can you see the patterns made with rectangles? Do you see a pattern made with horizontal lines?

:) ————————————————————

Do you see a pattern made with vertical lines?

M. C. Escher was an artist who used patterns to make **woodcuts.** Sometimes he repeated animal shapes in his artwork.

Look closely at the picture. What kinds of animals did Escher use to make the pattern? How are the birds different from the fish? Do you see patterns made with straight lines?

Can you see how the sky in the woodcut is different from the water? How do the animals in the pattern change?

M. C. Escher, *Sky and Water,* 1938. Woodcut.

When a circle is filled with color, it becomes a dot. People make fun clothes using fabrics with dot patterns.

Look at the clothes that you and your friends are wearing. What kinds of shapes and patterns do you see on the clothes?

There are many patterns found in nature. A black and white pattern covers a zebra's body.

Look closely at the zebra in the picture. Do you think its body is white with black lines? Or is it black with white lines?

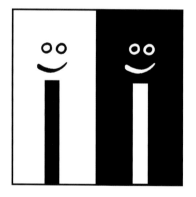

A snake is another animal with patterns on its body. The pattern of the snake's skin can tell you something very important! Do you know what that is?

This picture shows a poisonous sea snake from Indonesia. If you see a snake with this pattern, don't touch it!

This butterfly has colorful patterns on its wings. Are the patterns on its left wing the same as the patterns on its right wing?

Look at both pictures. Do you see patterns with thick lines? Do you see patterns with thin lines? Do you see dots on the butterfly's wings?

23

People can use lines and patterns to tell stories about nature. African artists use lines and patterns to create pictures on cloth. These pictures tell stories about animals and people.

Can you see the shapes and lines that are repeated to make a pattern? How many patterns can you see? Do you see white lines and black lines in the design?

Loopi can make the shape of a rectangle. Can you find patterns like this on the cloth?

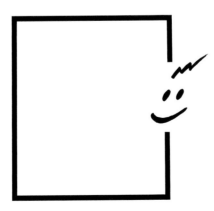

Pablo Picasso was an artist who used patterns in some of his paintings. He used many different colors in this **still life.**

There are many things to see in Picasso's painting. Can you find patterns made with the shape of a diamond?

Can you find patterns made with different kinds of lines?

Pablo Picasso, *Mandolin and Guitar,* 1924. Oil on canvas.

A quilt is a blanket made with shapes cut out of cloth. The shapes are repeated to create a pattern.

Different designs were used in this quilt. One design forms a star shape that looks like Loopi below. These designs form a pattern. How many star shapes can you count in the pattern? How many other shapes are there?

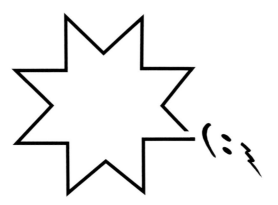

Dotty makes a diamond shape. Does the diamond shape form a pattern in the picture?

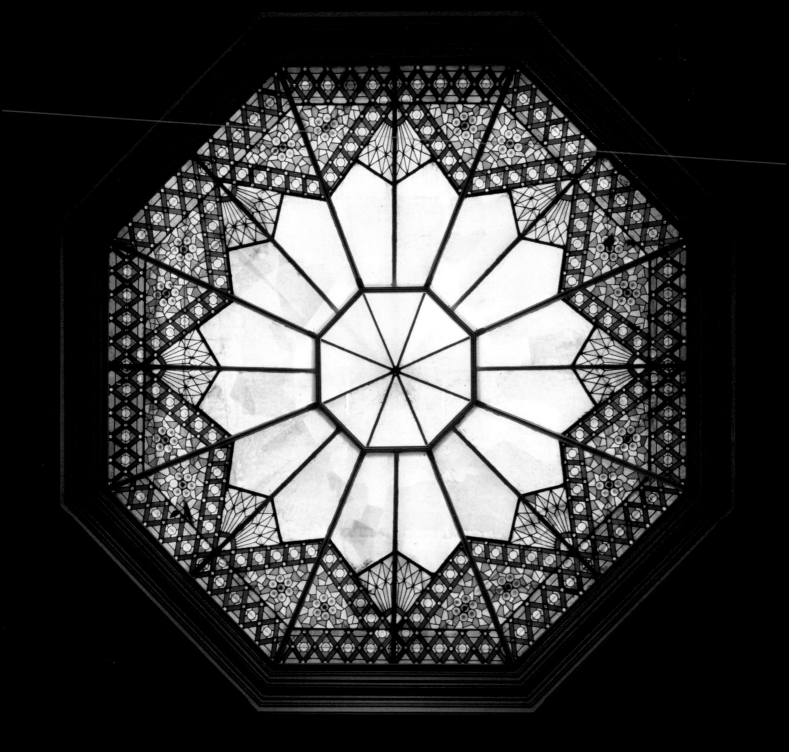

An artist makes a stained-glass window by putting shapes and colors together. When sun shines through the window, you can see a beautiful pattern.

30

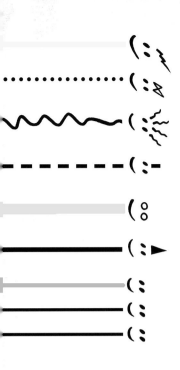

Put It All Together

Look at the picture of the window. Can you see the different shapes the artist used to create the pattern?

Make a Design for a Stained-Glass Window

Pretend you are making a pretty stained-glass window for your house. First you'll need to create a pattern design. Think of all the shapes and patterns you've learned about. Then draw the shapes so they touch each other. You can use straight lines or curved lines. Then add colors to your window design. Where will you put your window?

Students, Teachers, and Parents

LOOPI the Fantastic Line™ is always waiting to help you learn more about drawing with patterns—at www.scribblesinstitute.com. You can get helpful ideas for your drawings at the Scribbles Institute™. It's a great place for students, teachers, and parents to find books, information, and tips about drawing. You can even get advice from a drawing coach!

Glossary

arches (ARCH-ez)
Arches are curved shapes that form part of a building. An arch can form the top of a door, window, or gateway.

design (dih-ZINE)
A design is an arrangement of shapes and colors in a work of art. A design does not have to represent a person or thing.

sculpture (SKULP-cher)
A sculpture is a work of art formed into a shape to represent something. Sculptures can be carved from stone or made from metal.

still life (STILL LIFE)
A still life is a picture that shows nonliving things. A still life might show a bowl of fruit, for example.

woodcuts (WOOD-kuts)
A woodcut is a picture made from a block of wood with a design carved into it. The block is dipped in ink or paint and then pressed onto paper.

Index

About the Author
Rob Court is a designer and illustrator. He has a studio in San Juan Capistrano, California. He started the Scribbles Institute™ to help people learn about the importance of drawing and creativity.

This book is dedicated to Jesse and Jasmine.